Patriotic Holidays

BY
Cass R. Sandak

CRESTWOOD HOUSE
New York

Library of Congress Cataloging-in-Publication Data
Sandak, Cass R.
  Patriotic holidays

  p.   cm. – (Holidays)
  Includes bibliographical references.
  SUMMARY: Discusses the origins and traditions surrounding the Fourth of July, Presidents' Day,
Armistice Day, and other American holidays.
  1. Holidays—United States—Juvenile literature. 2. Heroes—United States—Juvenile literature.
3. United States—Social life and customs—Juvenile literature. [1. Holidays. 2. United States—Social
life and customs.] I. Title. II. Series: Holidays
GT4803.S26   1990   394.2'68473[S][WN]dc20   89-25380   CIP
ISBN 0-89686-501-0   AC

Photo Credits
Cover: Photo Researchers: Louis Goldman
DRK Photo: (Allan Kaye) 4; (Randy Trine) 10; (Annie Griffiths) 13, 36; (Tom Till) 17; (Stephen Krasemann)
   19, 21; (Tom Bean) 23; (D. Cavagnaro) 31; (Don & Pat Valenti) 38, 43; (Jim Brandenburg) 41
Culver Pictures, Inc.: 7, 8, 24, 27, 33, 35
FPG International: (Lawrence Schiller) 15
Journalism Services: (Joseph Jacobsen) 28

Macmillan Publishing Company
866 Third Avenue
New York, NY 10022
Collier Macmillan Canada, Inc.

CRESTWOOD HOUSE

Printed in the United States

First Edition

10 9 8 7 6 5 4 3 2 1

Contents

The Fourth of July

By all accounts it was one of the hottest summers ever. It was the summer of 1776. The place was Philadelphia, then the center of colonial government. The date was July 2. It was late in the afternoon in a building then known as the State House. It was soon to be renamed Independence Hall.

A very important idea was being considered. It was a resolution that the Second Continental Congress had introduced on June 7. It read, in part:

That these United Colonies are,
and of right ought to be, free
and independent states, that
they are absolved from
allegiance to the British Crown,
and that all political connection
between them and the state of
Great Britain is, and ought to be,
totally dissolved.

Many colonists were angry about what they saw as poor treatment by the British. They had decided to fight for more say in the way the government was run. War was raging all around the colonies on the eastern seaboard. The Revolutionary War had begun in 1775, when British and American soldiers had fought the Battle of Lexington and Concord in Massachusetts. Everyone present knew that if they voted for the resolution the war would go on. The war would last until the colonists knew they had won their independence.

Invented in Asia at least 800 years ago, firework displays have become an American Fourth of July tradition.

How the Resolution Was Created

Debate about the resolution raged on for almost a month. There were people from many colonies who felt that moving away from English rule would be a dangerous step. A unanimous vote was needed.

It had also taken several weeks to write the document that would set out, or declare, what the colonists wanted to do. Several weeks before, on June 10, the Continental Congress had chosen five men—Robert R. Livingston, Roger Sherman, Benjamin Franklin, John Adams, and Thomas Jefferson—to draft this declaration. No one is sure who wrote what parts of the document. One thing is certain, however. A large part of the text was written by Thomas Jefferson. The text became known as the Declaration of Independence.

On July 2, 1776, 12 of the 13 colonies voted for independence. On that day, the colonies became free and independent states. A new nation was born: the United States of America.

After the vote, the committee presented its resolution to the rest of the men at the meeting. A few words and statements in the declaration still had to be debated. This debate took two full days. It wasn't until July 4 that total agreement was reached and the colonists officially declared their independence.

What the Declaration Says

The Declaration of Independence is made up of four main parts. The first states the purpose of the document. It is called the preamble. The second part talks about the kind of government the new

6

The authors of the Declaration of Independence, from left to right: Thomas Jefferson, Roger Sherman, Benjamin Franklin, Robert R. Livingston, and John Adams

King George III of England, who ruled the American colonies
until they won their independence in 1776

8

country would have. It explains that power is to be in the hands of the people. This is probably the most famous part of the declaration. The third part lists complaints against King George III of England. The fourth part announces the separation.

One of the most famous passages near the beginning of the declaration reads:

> We hold these truths to be
> self-evident, that all men are
> created equal, that they are
> endowed by their Creator with
> certain unalienable rights, that
> among these are Life, Liberty,
> and the Pursuit of Happiness.

The first person to sign the declaration was John Hancock, the president of the Continental Congress. In fact, for a long time, Hancock's was the only signature on the document. At least one signature was needed to make the document legal, and his became the first. He wrote his signature in large letters. He said he wanted George III to be able to read the name without his spectacles! To this day, to "put your John Hancock" on a piece of paper means to sign your name.

On July 6, the document was reproduced for the first time in a newspaper, the *Pennsylvania Evening Post*. At noon on July 8, it was read to the public for the first time in Philadelphia's Independence Square. Then a great bell was rung. Originally known as the Province Bell, it was soon renamed the Liberty Bell.

On July 9, the document was read for the first time in New York. On the 18th, the people of Boston first heard it. There it was read from the balcony of the State House. Cannons roared 13 times, and soldiers fired rifles 13 times—once for each colony. In many places, the colonists destroyed statues of George III and burned portraits of him.

The colonists then made a parchment copy of the declaration and put the first signature on it on August 2. It took a few weeks more to add all the signatures. Finally there would be 56 signers. Then the document was complete and in the form we know it today.

Since the first official Fourth of July celebration in 1777, fireworks have been a colorful part of this patriotic holiday.

How the Fourth Is Celebrated

The first official Fourth of July celebration occurred in 1777, one year after the exciting event in Philadelphia. John Adams argued that July 2–the day the colonists voted for independence–should have been the day for celebration. Others thought it should be on the day independence was officially declared. So July 4 was the day agreed upon. In Philadelphia, bells rang out and guns were shot off. At night, there were bonfires and fireworks. Soldiers on duty nearby were given an extra measure of rum to celebrate the day. Congress gave a dinner for city officials and military officers who were stationed nearby. Bands played, and decorated pieces of cloth, known as bunting, was displayed.

In 1788, the celebration in Philadelphia was larger than it had ever been before. That year, there was a new reason for celebration. The Constitution of the new country had been ratified, or approved, in September 1787, the year before. People formed a huge parade to show that there was even more to feel patriotic about.

By about 1810, most cities acknowledged the Fourth of July as a national holiday. The holiday was popular in the South, but was not celebrated during the Civil War. In Boston, Massachusetts, July 4 was not celebrated until much later. The people of Boston instead held Patriots' Day to honor the start of the Battle of Lexington and Concord. It wasn't until 1883 that Bostonians joined the rest of the nation in celebrating the Fourth of July.

Independence Day first came to California about the same time as the gold rush opened up the western part of the country. The tiny town of Los Angeles had its first celebration in 1847.

A few years later, in 1876, the country's 100th birthday stirred up more patriotism. Many celebrations were held honoring the country's centennial. During this celebration, Alexander Graham Bell introduced the telephone in Philadelphia. That's where the Centennial Exposition, much like a world's fair, was located. More than ten million people came to celebrate.

Many of these people saw the actual Declaration of Independence on display at the fair. The document was beginning to show its age. Careful sealing and lighting have helped to preserve it. Since 1924, the declaration has been on display in the National Archives Building in Washington, D.C.

July 4, often called Independence Day, is a legal holiday in all states and in all U.S. territories overseas. It is one of the few holidays that has not been moved to the nearest Friday or Monday to make a three-day weekend. No matter what day of the week July 4 falls on, it is celebrated on that day. Since the day is in the middle of summer, when most schools are closed, it has become a time for family and community get-togethers. July 4 is the most honored nonreligious holiday in America. This is because it stands for the birth of freedom, the birth of our nation.

Patriotism means many things to many people. The word comes from the Latin *patria*, which means "homeland" or "fatherland." For most of us, it also means love of country, a special feeling that comes from knowing what the original founders believed.

Perhaps the most exciting of all Fourth of July parties came in 1976, when the country celebrated its 200th birthday. This bicentennial party featured 212 sailing ships in New York Harbor. The "tall" ships had sailed from more than 30 different nations to parade up the Hudson River. Thousands of visitors from all over the world came to watch the impressive sight.

President Gerald Ford was on board a navy aircraft carrier and rang the ship's bell 13 times. This was a symbolic salute to the original 13 colonies. In Philadelphia, a few special people were allowed to ring the Liberty Bell. They were descendants of the original signers of the Declaration of Independence. They could

12   On July 4, 1986, hundreds of small boats and tall ships sailed into New York Harbor to celebrate the 100th birthday of the Statue of Liberty.

only tap it gently, for the great bell has been cracked for more than 200 years. In Washington, D.C., more than two million people watched one of the largest fireworks displays ever.

In 1986, another thrilling Fourth of July happened. The occasion was the 100th birthday of the Statue of Liberty in New York Harbor. The statue was a gift from the French government. It had been closed for repair for several years, and this July 4 marked the relighting of Miss Liberty. Special stamps and coins were issued, and a new group of tall ships sailed through the harbor. The grand finale to the week-long festivities included elaborate fireworks displays. For years, the statue's beacon, at the entrance to this great city, has been a symbol for Americans returning to their country. More than that, it has held the light to welcome many immigrants who have come to live in the United States.

Martin Luther King's Day

The newest American holiday has been observed only since 1986. In that year, Congress voted to celebrate the birthday of civil rights leader Martin Luther King, Jr. King's birthday is January 30, but the third Monday in January has been declared the legal holiday, or the day it is officially celebrated.

Reverend Martin Luther King, Jr., was an African-American born in 1929 in Atlanta, Georgia. While he was growing up, he saw the ways American blacks in the South were suffering. Many of them were not allowed to vote. Blacks had to drink from separate drinking fountains and go to separate schools. And the only seats on buses they could use were the ones in the back.

A deeply religious man, King wanted to show that conditions could improve. Nonviolence was important to King. In many ways,

With his powerful speeches and unfailing commitment to racial equality, Martin Luther King, Jr., helped African-Americans win political freedom.

King followed the philosophy of India's Mohandas Gandhi. Gandhi had used nonviolence to protest his country's unjust laws.

In 1963, Martin Luther King, Jr., made an important speech. It began with the words "I have a dream." He dreamed that someday there would be freedom and justice for all Americans. He delivered the speech during a civil rights march in Washington, D.C. During the march, protesters demanded for all people the right to vote and to be educated.

In 1964, King received the Nobel Peace Prize for his work in improving race relations. He is also the author of six books, many of which deal with civil rights topics.

Ironically, this peaceful man's life came to a violent end in 1968. An assassin's bullet killed him in Memphis, Tennessee. But his legacy remains. His work has been carried on by other black leaders, including his widow, Coretta Scott King.

Presidents' Day

Presidents' Day is a new holiday, too. It honors two of the greatest American presidents, George Washington and Abraham Lincoln. Their birthdays used to be celebrated separately. Since both birthdays fall in February, a joint holiday to honor both men was proposed. Presidents' Day comes on the third Monday in February, and it is a legal holiday in most states. Some places, however, still celebrate the old holidays.

Abraham Lincoln's birthday, February 12, is a legal holiday in most western and northern states. Lincoln's term of office spanned the years of the War Between the States, or the Civil War. Even now, 12 southern states continue to celebrate Robert E. Lee's birthday on January 19, instead of Lincoln's. Lee was leader of the Confederate Army during the Civil War. Jefferson Davis's birthday on June 3 is celebrated as well in some places in the South. Davis was the president of the Confederacy during the Civil War.

Lincoln was the 16th president of the United States. His leadership of the country and the victories of the Union army managed to keep the nation united at a very perilous time. Lincoln was assassinated just a few days before the Civil War ended. He was shot on April 14, 1865, while he and his wife were watching a performance at Ford's Theater in Washington.

Lincoln's Birthday was celebrated as a holiday for the first time on February 12, 1866, ten months after his death. Observance of the day was regional. In Jersey City, New Jersey, a group calling themselves the Lincoln Association met. Ten years later, the first of many statues erected in his memory appeared in Washington, D.C. In 1892, Lincoln's home state of Illinois became the first to make his birthday a legal holiday. In 1909, special celebrations were held on Lincoln's 100th birthday. In 1959, on the occasion of the 150th anniversary of his birth, there were even more elaborate festivities.

As a result of those celebrations, Lincoln became better known and more popular. Perhaps the most famous tribute to the great man's memory began on Lincoln's Birthday in 1914. This was the date of the groundbreaking of the Lincoln Memorial, near the banks of the Potomac River in Washington, D.C. The great marble building took eight years to complete—at a cost of $3 million. It wasn't finished until 1922 and was dedicated on Lincoln's Birthday. One of the most famous parts of the memorial is the seated statue of Lincoln. The work was done by the noted sculptor Daniel Chester French. Since 1960, U.S. pennies, known as Lincoln pennies, have shown a view of the Lincoln Memorial on one side. On the other side is Lincoln's well-known profile.

*　　*　　*

The Lincoln Memorial in Washington, D.C., casts a peaceful reflection. It reminds people of the president who guided the country through the Civil War and ended slavery in America.

George Washington was commander in chief of the First American Army. After the United States won the Revolutionary War against England, Washington was unanimously chosen the first president of the United States.

George Washington's birth date was February 22, 1732. Washington was actually born on February 11, according to the old-style calendar. This calendar wasn't changed until after Washington's birth. The date of Washington's birthday was officially changed in 1790. By this time, everyone was so confused that for many years people continued to celebrate on both days.

George Washington is one of the few people in history whose birthday was publicly celebrated while he was alive. This came from the English and European tradition of celebrating the monarch's birthday. There is a record of the public celebration of Washington's birthday on February 11, 1781, 18 years before his death! A parade of troops marched in Newport, Rhode Island, to mark the day. In 1791, a military parade was held in Washington's honor in Philadelphia. That same year, plans for the nation's capital—Washington, D.C.—were laid out. After our first president died in 1799, Congress declared that the 1800 observation of Washington's birthday should be a national day of mourning.

People often make cherry pies or log-shaped cakes topped with chocolate icing and cherries on Washington's Birthday. These traditional foods refer to the story of young George Washington mischievously chopping down a cherry tree. When his father caught him, young George is said to have told him: "I cannot tell a lie." The story is well known, but most likely the event never took place. Parson Mason L. Weems, who wrote one of the first biographies of Washington, probably made the story up to illustrate young George's integrity.

When Washington died in December 1799, he was buried in a tomb at Mount Vernon, his estate in the Virginia countryside near

18 Cherry trees bloom in front of the Washington Monument, the 555-foot-tall tower that pays tribute to the nation's first president.

Washington, D.C. More than half a million people go to Washington's tomb yearly. For many years it was said to be the most visited shrine in the country.

Large celebrations on Washington's 100th birthday were held in 1832, especially in Boston, Massachusetts. On his 200th birthday in 1932, the celebrations were bigger than ever. Commemorative stamps were issued and special programs were sponsored. Major ceremonies were held at historic spots around the country that claimed some connection with Washington.

By that time, many places had been named or renamed in honor of the country's first president. Washington's name appears throughout the country: It is the name of the nation's capital, a state, and several cities, counties, and towns. Not far from the Lincoln Memorial in Washington, D.C., stands the Washington Monument. It is a 555-foot-high beacon made from Vermont granite. The monument towers over the rest of the city. Begun in 1848, it was finished in 1885. One of the reasons the monument took so long to finish is that no work was done on it from 1854 to 1880! Lack of public funds was one reason. The Civil War was another.

Although Lincoln and Washington had two very different personalities, their dreams and beliefs were similar. They both believed strongly in the union of the country. It is appropriate that their birthdays have become linked in recent years through Presidents' Day.

Arlington National Cemetery is the site of one of the most moving Memorial Day celebrations in the country. Heroes from every war in which America fought are buried there.

Memorial Day

No one is quite sure when and where Memorial Day was first celebrated. The evidence points to Boalsburg, a small town in Pennsylvania. Soon after the end of the Civil War, several women banded together there. They were wives and mothers of soldiers who had died in the war. They met to decorate the graves of their husbands and sons with flowers and wreaths. By May 30, 1869, this yearly custom had become an established tradition. As early as 1873, the day was declared a legal holiday in New York. In 1971, however, the date for Memorial Day was changed to the last Monday in May.

For many years, the day was called Decoration Day. In 1882, the Grand Army of the Republic suggested changing the name to Memorial Day. In Virginia, the same day is known as Confederate Memorial Day. In several southern states, June 3, Jefferson Davis's birthday, is observed as a Memorial Day for Confederate soldiers.

Memorial Day celebrations may include parades with marching bands and speakers. People often gather to honor the war dead. They may dedicate a monument or place a wreath at a particular grave or shrine. Or they may present a gift or donation to some patriotic organization. Over the years, the day has changed to include honoring all people who have died, not just those killed in battle.

Some families gather for prayers at grave sites on Memorial Day. It has become a day to remember any dead friends and family members. In this way, it resembles the Greek and Roman tradition of honoring the dead with flowers or branches on certain days.

Many people still decorate graves with flowers or shrubs. There may be even more elaborate ceremonies. At Gettysburg Memorial Park, in Pennsylvania, there is a service of remembrance to mark a major battle during the Civil War.

Perhaps the most impressive ceremony is the one that takes place at Arlington National Cemetery in Virginia, where a wreath is laid at the Tomb of the Unknowns. This place is the site where servicemen and women from all American wars are honored. The wreath is placed there by an honor guard of the armed forces as bands play solemn music.

In 1984, the latest unknown warrior was brought to Arlington to be laid to rest. The remains of this soldier, a victim of the Vietnam War, were brought to the tomb, which used to be called the Tomb of the Unknown Soldier. He joined three other symbolic warriors, one each from World War I, World War II, and the Korean War. On Memorial Day 1984, the resting place was renamed the Tomb of the Unknowns.

Memorial Day is observed in every country where American warriors are buried. Flags on government buildings and on some ships throughout the world fly at half-mast on Memorial Day as a tribute to the dead.

Another important Memorial Day site is the Vietnam War Memorial. This long black granite wall near the Washington Monument is engraved with the names of all the men and women who died fighting in Southeast Asia.

A drawing of an early Labor Day parade

Labor Day

Labor Day began only about a hundred years ago in New York City. Since it is the first Monday in September, it marks the traditional end of summer. Schools often open the day after Labor Day, although in some places classes begin the week before the holiday. Labor Day is a legal holiday, a day when all offices close and most workers are given the day off. Some cities have parades, and families and groups hold picnics.

A hundred years ago, working conditions were very different than they are today. Most people worked at least six days a week and some worked seven. Sometimes they worked as many as 12 to 14 hours each day. Working conditions were often unsafe. Wages were low. In many families, children went to work at the ages of 11 or 12. In some, children as young as 5 or 6 often worked the same hours and under the same poor conditions as adults.

In the 1880s, workers began to band together. They formed organizations called labor unions. Workers adopted the motto "In union there is strength." A labor union could be helpful in bringing about

24

needed changes to the laws concerning workers. Often each group of workers—such as miners or seamstresses—had its own union. A worker joined the one for his or her profession.

Unions had been operating for many years in Europe. In Europe, these unions, or guilds, often had their own holidays. May 1 had become the traditional day for European workers to celebrate. This date had been a holiday since the Middle Ages. It was adopted as the standard workers' holiday, especially by communists.

The first laborers' day was celebrated in America when the Central Labor Union of New York declared it would hold a great labor festival on Monday, September 5, 1882. The Central Labor Union was a group of small unions that had banded together. The suggestion was put forth by Peter McGuire, a member of the Knights of Labor. The site they chose was New York City's Union Square.

When the first Labor Day parade started, it looked as though it would not be a success. Few people turned out to march in it or to observe the workers filing by. But as the parade marched on, it gathered momentum. Gradually, bands and groups of union members from different trades swelled the ranks. Soon, 10,000 people were marching through the streets of New York City! Some of the workers carried signs calling for reforms such as shorter hours and better pay.

Later, 50,000 workers and their families gathered in a park for a picnic lunch. There were speeches and fireworks. The first Labor Day had turned out to be a huge success.

By 1889, 400 American cities were celebrating Labor Day. In 1894, President Grover Cleveland asked for Labor Day to be made a legal holiday. Oregon was the first state to pass a law declaring the holiday a legal one. Soon Colorado, New York, New Jersey, and Massachusetts followed. By the 1930s, Labor Day had become a legal holiday in every state.

Thanks to the efforts of workers in the labor movement, working conditions and wages today are much fairer than they were on the first Labor Day.

Columbus Day

October 12 is a day to honor the achievements of Christopher Columbus—the first European to discover the Americas. Today, this legal holiday occurs on the second Monday in October. October 12, 1492, is the date Columbus landed for the first time in the New World. No one knows for sure exactly where Columbus landed, but it is generally believed that he set foot first on Watling Island in the Bahamas.

An Italian explorer, Columbus went to sea as a young man and sailed around the ports of Europe for many years. He also studied mapmaking in Lisbon, then the center of navigation studies. Columbus was sure the Earth was round, not flat. He believed that by sailing west, he would still come to the east. He also thought the journey would only be a few thousand miles. In the east he would reach the Indies, and possibly even China and Japan.

Any journey would be an expensive one, so Columbus searched among the rulers of Europe for financial help to make his voyage. After a 14-year struggle, King Ferdinand and Queen Isabella of Spain gave him the backing he needed as well as the ships. The *Niña, Pinta,* and *Santa Maria* were the vessels that carried Columbus and his crew of about a hundred men to America.

Columbus made many major discoveries in the New World, including exotic plants that could be eaten, strange and colorful birds, and dark-skinned people he called "Indians." On a total of four voyages, he discovered the islands of Trinidad, Hispaniola, Jamaica, and Cuba. He landed in several countries of Central America and even touched the coast of mainland South America.

The first Columbus Day was celebrated on October 12, 1792, 300 years after the famous voyage. But it wasn't until a hundred years later, in 1892, that the holiday was observed again. In 1893, the

In this painting, an elegantly dressed Christopher Columbus sets foot in the New World for the first time.

Columbian Exposition opened in Chicago to commemorate the 400th anniversary of Columbus's discovery. This was a world's fair exposition that drew people from all over the world. Today, Columbus Day is a legal holiday in most parts of North and South America. It is celebrated with colorful parades in many large cities.

Veterans' Day

Veterans' Day was once called Armistice Day. But since 1954, the holiday has been known as Veterans' Day. The original holiday honored the armistice, or cease-fire agreement, signed on November 11, 1918. This cease-fire ended World War I. The war did not officially end until 1919, when the Treaty of Versailles was signed. Since then, several other wars have been fought. So now the holiday honors the veterans of those wars, too. Today, Veterans' Day is celebrated on November 11. It is a legal holiday in most states.

The first Armistice Day celebration was held on November 11, 1919, the anniversary of the signing of the armistice. For many years, the celebrations included a tradition of observing two minutes of silence at the same hour that the fighting had stopped: 11 A.M. This was the 11th hour of the 11th day of the 11th month!

In 1920, both France and England first celebrated the day–and still do. In England and Canada, Armistice Day is now called Remembrance Day. Belgium–where so much of World War I was fought–honors the day as well.

On Armistice Day in 1921, the United States buried the unknown soldier. Chosen from four unmarked graves in France, the soldier's remains were brought back to the United States. The body was buried at the Tomb of the Unknown Soldier in Arlington National Cemetery. The inscription on the tomb reads:

Here rests in honored glory
An American Soldier
Known but to God

On November 11, 1921, the day the unknown soldier was buried, Armistice Day became an official holiday. Each year at Arlington,

A guard stands watch at the Tomb of the Unknowns, a monument built to honor soldiers killed in battle.

the president or his representative places a wreath at the Tomb of the Unknowns.

Until 1938, Armistice Day was an official holiday by presidential proclamation. On the 20th anniversary, it became a legal holiday. In 1954, an act of Congress renamed the day to include veterans of World War II and the Korean War.

Other National or Patriotic Holidays

Inauguration Day

Inauguration Day occurs only in years after presidential elections and takes place on January 20. On this day, the president of the United States is sworn into office. It is a legal holiday only in Washington, D.C., where the inauguration is held. Originally inaugurations were held on March 4. But in 1933, the ceremony was moved forward to January, as provided by the 20th Amendment to the Constitution.

The most important part of the day is the ceremony during which the president is given the oath of office from the chief justice of the Supreme Court. This is usually done on a large platform built on the east side of the Capitol building. Following this, there is a big parade down Pennsylvania Avenue to the White House. Many people attend glittering inaugural balls held on that evening and sometimes on the evenings before and after the inauguration. The celebration of the inauguration of John Fitzgerald Kennedy in 1961 lasted three days.

Arbor Day

Arbor Day began on the treeless plains of Nebraska. In 1872, J. Sterling Morton established the first tree-planting day. His idea was to plant trees as a conservation measure, primarily to keep the

Students in California plant gardens in honor of Luther Burbank, a famous naturalist, on Arbor Day.

soil in place. Under his direction, more than one million trees were planted that day. In the time since, billions of trees have been planted during Arbor Day celebrations throughout the country. The tradition may go back to the Aztecs of ancient Mexico. They said a tree should be planted when a child was born. The custom is still observed in modern Mexico and in Spain, where it is called *Fiesta del Arbol* (Tree Festival).

Arbor Day is not a legal holiday, but most states observe it in some way. In many parts of the country, Arbor Day is a popular school and civic celebration. Groups encourage people to improve the landscape by planting trees. The holiday has no firm date, but instead depends on the local climate. Some places choose March or April as good planting months. In Florida, where cold weather is not a consideration, Arbor Day is held in January! Nebraska celebrates Morton's birthday, April 22. And in California, Arbor Day is celebrated on the birthday of the naturalist Luther Burbank.

Pan-American Day

Pan-American Day has been celebrated since 1931 on April 14. The day honors the 21 North, Central, and South American republics. Originally, the holiday was intended to promote good relations among the New World republics. Although it is not a legal holiday, Pan-American Day is often celebrated in schools and by civic and multiethnic groups.

Patriots' Day

In Maine and Massachusetts, the third Monday in April is called Patriots' Day. It is a legal holiday in those states. The day has been set aside to remember the men and women who risked their lives to establish our country. The date is usually close to April 18. This is

Patriots' Day is celebrated on or near April 18, the day on which Paul Revere warned Americans that the fight for independence would soon begin.

the anniversary of Paul Revere's midnight ride to warn colonists of the British invasion. The invasion led to the Battle of Lexington and Concord on April 19, 1775. The Revolutionary War began with that battle.

Armed Forces Day

Armed Forces Day honors members of the army, navy, and air force of the United States. It occurs on the third Saturday in May. Originally, each branch of the services had its own day to commemorate. In 1947, however, the days were combined. Armed

Forces Day is a day set aside by the U.S. government. It acknowledges the role of men and women of the armed services in safeguarding the welfare of our country. Parades and special programs by the three branches of the armed services mark the day. If there is a military base nearby, there is likely to be a big parade. Jets fly overhead in formation. Military vessels are open for inspection. There may even be programs to show off new equipment to the public.

Flag Day

June 14, 1777, was the day the Continental Congress adopted a resolution to prepare a flag for the new republic. Now June 14 honors the Stars and Stripes. The holiday did not become official until 1949, when President Harry S Truman issued the proclamation.

Sometimes the American flag is also referred to affectionately as Old Glory. Each part of the flag and each color have special meaning. The stars, of course, represent each state in the Union. They are set in a blue background like the stars in heaven. The red stripes, which represent England, are separated by bands of white. The number of stripes has always been 13. This symbolizes the original 13 colonies. Because the number of states has grown to 50, however, the numbers—and arrangements—of stars has changed each time a new state was added.

There is a well-known story about the origin of the flag. It says that George Washington went to the Philadelphia home of seamstress Betsy Ross. He asked her to make a flag that would be right for the new country. Although this story has become part of American folklore, there is no proof that it ever happened. In fact, the name of

According to legend, Betsy Ross, a Philadelphia seamstress, was asked by George Washington to make the country's first flag.

Betsy Ross was not known at all until about 1870, when her grandson told the story. The only thing anyone knows for sure is that Betsy Ross did exist. And she was, indeed, the official flag maker for the U.S. Navy.

The first Flag Day celebration occurred on June 14, 1877, on the 100th birthday of the flag. In 1894, a group got together and formed a special Flag Day Association. The American flag has the distinction of being the only flag that has had a national anthem written about it. Its title is "The Star-Spangled Banner." The words for the song were written by Francis Scott Key in 1814, during the War of 1812.

At this special naturalization ceremony, held on July 4, 1986, the famous Russian dancer Mikhail Baryshnikov became an American citizen.

Citizenship Day

Citizenship Day combines two earlier American celebrations. They are Constitution Day and "I Am an American" Day. It is celebrated on September 17, the date the Constitution was first signed at Independence Hall in 1787. Constitution Day originally commemorated that event. "I Am an American" Day is a day that celebrates citizenship, especially for people who were born in other lands and became United States citizens by the naturalization process. Now the holiday honors the document that gave America its democratic government and congratulates people who have gained the right to vote and hold government office. It is not a legal holiday, but it is important to many people.

United Nations Day

United Nations Day is celebrated on October 24. This is the anniversary of the founding of the United Nations (UN) in 1945. Following the horrible years of World War II, world leaders met in San Francisco to discuss the need for an international organization that would maintain world peace. The United Nations charter that created the organization was written and signed in 1945. It wasn't until 1948, however, that the first United Nations Day was celebrated. It is not a legal holiday, but it is observed in many ways. In recent years, a UN Day Concert has been televised nationwide. Held at the United Nations headquarters in New York City, the concert generally features well-known classical musicians from many countries around the world.

Two citizens cast their votes behind the curtains of voting booths on Election Day.

Election Day

Election Day is the first Tuesday after the first Monday in November. Since 1845, it has been the day for electing the president and vice president. The presidential election occurs every four years, starting from the first year of a century. In 1872, congressional representatives were added to the ballot. Now citizens vote for people to fill offices in local governments. They also voice their opinions on certain major new laws. Each state determines which elections are held in nonpresidential years. The presidential election years are the only years in which the holiday is a legal one.

International Patriotic Holidays

Many countries around the world celebrate their own independence days. Perhaps the most famous occurs in France. Every year on July 14, the French observe Bastille Day. This celebrates the day in 1789 that citizens stormed the Bastille, a prison in Paris. With that attack began the French Revolution, which eventually freed the people of France from the rule of kings and queens. In 1989, the celebration of Bastille Day was particularly stirring. Many world leaders gathered to honor the people of France on the 200th anniversary of their freedom.

Canada celebrates its independence on Dominion Day. This occurs on July 1 and commemorates the day in 1867 when Canada became a dominion in the British Commonwealth. That means it received the right to make its own laws and decide how to spend taxes. But it still recognizes the British queen as the head of government.

In Mexico, Independence Day is observed on September 16. On that day in 1810, a priest named Hidalgo asked fellow Mexicans to declare their independence from Spanish rule. For more than ten years, Mexico was torn by revolution and strife. But its dream of independence finally came true.

In the Soviet Union, two days, November 7 and 8, mark the overthrow of the czars and the beginning of the Russian Revolution. These days are known as Revolution Days. Because it is a Communist country, the Soviet Union also observes May 1 as a workers' day. The latest military machines are shown to the Soviet people in huge parades, some of which last for two days.

In India, August 15 marks Independence Day. On that day in 1947, British rule was overthrown. India, like Canada, became an independent dominion. Another day important to people in India is Republic Day, celebrated on January 26. This is the day, first observed in 1950, when India threw over its dominion status and became completely independent.

* * *

Wherever people love their homelands and cherish the stories of their nations' histories, there are patriotic holidays. The Fourth of July is one of the best known of these holidays. To many people, it means picnics, baseball games, and fireworks. More than that, however, it means freedom.

On Dominion Day, Canadians celebrate winning their
independence from England. Here, the Royal Canadian
Mounted Police, better known as Mounties, gather for a
ceremony in Alberta.

Holiday Trivia

July 4 is a famous date in American history for many reasons:

Even before the United States became an independent nation, July 4 was important in our history. Roger Williams founded the colony of Rhode Island on July 4, 1636.

In 1777, Admiral John Paul Jones raised the Stars and Stripes over his ship, the *Ranger*.

July 4, 1802, marked the opening day of the U.S. Military Academy at West Point.

The Erie Canal was begun on July 4, 1817.

The Baltimore and Ohio Railroad was begun on this historic date in 1828.

Near the end of the Civil War, the city of Vicksburg surrendered on July 4, 1863.

On July 4, 1960, the first American flag to bear 50 stars was raised. This celebrated Hawaii's entrance into the Union as the country's 50th state.

Some famous people share July 4 as their birthdays:

Nathaniel Hawthorne, author of *The House of Seven Gables* and *The Scarlet Letter*, in 1804.

Calvin Coolidge, the 30th president of the United States, in 1872.

Stephen Collins Foster, songwriter and composer of *Camptown Races* and *Jeannie with the Light Brown Hair*, among others, in 1826.

Giuseppe Garibaldi, the Italian patriot, in 1807. Although he was an Italian, Garibaldi lived for several years in the United States.

In addition, two former presidents of the United States both died on the same July 4. They were John Adams and Thomas Jefferson. The year? 1826. Our fifth president, James Monroe, also died on a July 4, but in 1831.

There's an interesting story about how the name Old Glory came to stand for the country's flag. Captain William Driver, of Salem,

Whether it is called "Old Glory" or the "Stars and Stripes," the American flag is the best-known symbol of patriotism in the country.

Massachusetts, was about to make a round-the-world voyage in 1824. Several women from his town presented him with a huge flag they had made. As he raised it, he shouted, ''Old Glory! Old Glory!'' and the tradition has stuck.

One of the most famous symbols of America's fight for independence, the Liberty Bell, is also famous for the great crack in its side. This occurred shortly after the bell was made. While it was being tested in 1750, the break appeared. Everyone has treated it very carefully ever since.

For Further Reading

Burnett, Bernice. *The First Book of Holidays*. Revised ed. New York: Franklin Watts, 1955, 1974.

Commager, Henry Steele. *The Great Declaration: A Book for Young Americans*. Indianapolis, Indiana: The Bobbs-Merrill Company Inc., 1958.

Grigoli, Valorie. *Patriotic Holidays and Celebrations. A First Book*. New York: Franklin Watts, 1985.

Ickis, Marguerite. *The Book of Patriotic Holidays*. New York: Dodd, Mead & Co., 1962.

Krythe, Maymie R. *All about American Holidays*. New York: Harper and Brothers, 1962.

Peterson, Helen Stone. *Give Us Liberty: The Story of the Declaration of Independence*. Champaign, Ill.; Garrard Publishing Company, 1973.

Sechrist, Elizabeth Hough. *Red Letter Days, A Book of Holiday Customs*. Revised ed. Philadelphia: Macrae Smith Company, 1940, 1965.

Index